ABC *of* TRANSLATION

Poems & Drawings

Willis Barnstone

ABC *of* TRANSLATION

Poems & Drawings

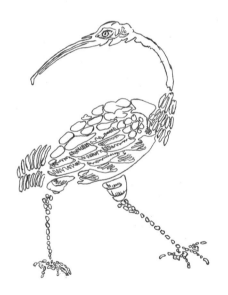

Black Widow Press is an imprint of Commonwealth Books, Inc., Boston, MA. Distributed to the trade by NBN (National Book Network) throughout North America, Canada, and the U.K. All Black Widow Press books are printed on acid-free paper, and glued into bindings. Black Widow Press and its logo are registered trademarks of Commonwealth Books, Inc.

Joseph S. Phillips and Susan J. Wood, Ph.D, Publishers
www.blackwidowpress.com

All illustrations by Willis Barnstone
Text Design: Willis Barnstone
Cover Design & Production: Kerrie Kemperman

ISBN-13: 978-0-9837079-2-9

Printed in the United States

10 9 8 7 6 5 4 3 2 1

for James Laughlin

Inventor of Books & Dylan Thomas

Ruth Stone

Creator of Galaxies

Gerald Stern

Author of Ecclesiastes

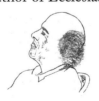

Stanley Moss

Inventor of Poetry

ACKNOWLEDGMENTS

Sweet Briar College published a pamphlet, *ABC of Translation* (1990), based on a lecture given there. Later the poet and publisher James Laughlin suggested I end my *The Poetics of Translation: History, Theory, Practice,* with an ABC on translation. This present book is an expanded version of those final pages in *The Poetics of Translation: History, Theory, Practice,* Yale University Press, 1993

I think of close friends and companions in translation who have enriched world literature. Tony Kerrigan recreated the poetry and prose of Borges for our age; Norman Shapiro, a colleague at Wesleyan is an inventor in English of Gautier, Baudelaire, Verlaine, La Fontaine, and centuries of women's poetry; Martín Hadis in Argentina keeps Borges's secrets alive in books and articles; and generous Edwin Honig knighted in Portugal and Spain for volumes on Pessoa, Lope de Vega, Calderón de la Barca, and Lorca. In his unique work on translation, *The Poet's Other Voice,* twelve writers chat about translation. The phrases I like most are, "It's impossible, of course — that's why I do it," from Willard Trask, and "I prefer the live dog over the dead lion," from Robert Fitzgerald.

I wish to thank Elli Barnstone, with whom I first translated the Greek novel, *The Other Alexander* by Margarita Liberaki, for her expert eye on ancient Greek lyric poetry and Greek gospels. I am always cheered by my daughter Aliki Barnstone's *The Collected Poems of C.P. Cavafy,* Norton, 2006, and son Tony Barnstone's *Anchor Book of Chinese Poetry,* Anchor, 2005. My deep appreciation goes to my wife Sarah Handler, author of *Austere Luminosity of Chinese Classical Furniture,* University of California Press, 2001, who has read and helped me on each page of this book.

CONTENTS

ART

Orphan in an Alien City

Translation is
        the **art** of **revelation.**
                The poet translator recognizes,

recreates, and thereby
        reveals the original
            artist's work.

The picaresque volume
        floats off to mystery
            of possible esteem

or normal starvation.
        The winds of chance howl.
            Though famous at home,

in a new tongue
        the book is an orphan
            in an alien city. With no past

the newcomer
        may become myth.
            In rags or hand me downs

or pretended glory,
        the newly dressed orphan
                is morning surprise to crowds.

He is a distinctive stranger.
        The orphan is Don Quijote de la Mancha
        in Chicago.

Borges's Mad Ménard

A New Vision of Authorship

In his famous tale, *Pierre Ménard, Author of the Quijote*, a spoof parable of a philosophy of translation gone astray, Borges makes a Frenchman author of a Golden Age novel by virtue of his pioneer theory of translation. Ménard, a modern civilized French man of letters, in meticulous elegant Gallic penmanship produces pages that coincide — word for word and line for line — with a few chapters of *Don Quijote*. His fragmentary *Don Quijote* trumps Cervantes who indulges in a coarse opposition between knighthood and the provincial reality of his country. Ménard's "reality" is the land of guitars and dancing Carmen.

Think of Ménard's version of *Don Quijote* as a palimpsest below which the Cervantes text is a bloated draft. Pierre's handwritten Spanish document is free of error, icily perfect, rational, and infinitely richer than the printed rubble of baroque Miguel de Cervantes, the barbaric one-armed 7th-century Spaniard.

M. Pierre Ménard, a punctilious copyright felon, never blunders into the messy imperfect act of translating between tongues. Pierre assumed the magisterial role of the unpaid Greek slave copyists in Rome, the *librarii*, who selflessly copy works of Lucretius, Epicurus, and Plato for later generations.

Borges keeps Ménard mercilessly busy copying line for line the original picaresque Spanish novel into Spanish. Ultimately, the revolutionary Parisian scholar dethrones crude commoner Cervantes, son of a *Jewish* surgeon and a mere soldier who fought in the Battle of Lepanto. Parisian Ménard becomes the author king of *Don Quijote*.

As a hero and master of enlightened modernity, the Catholic genius invents a true reader-response theory with no obscure rant of the circumcised American academicians. With supreme idiocy, perfect Pierre brags of victory.

Between

Hop Nations and Hear a New Song

Translation is an art of hopping **between** tongues,
The child of this art lives forever between home
       and a foreign planet.
   Once across the border, in new garb,

the orphan remembers or conceals the old town
and appears newborn and different with new sounds,
       prosody, and grammar.
   Translation tolerates no mirrors.

Between tongues there are no perfect equivalents.
   Hop nations and hear a song in new colors.
      A Spanish *luna* peering
      over Granada's snow mountains

is not an English *moon* emerging from London smog.
How different William Blake's patient *sunflower*
      from Lorca's *girasol,*
      "the turning sun!" The Englishman's

sunflower weary of time seeks a golden clime
for the Virgin in her grave. Lorca's turning
      sun blooms and spins
     a gold horse in a gypsy's eyeball.

Clown

Dress Him in Hamlet's Cape

O mad and harmful dream of perfection!

Whether the child is amazingly like its parents
or wears not only a new costume but a new face and lips
to sing and laugh in echoes in another land,
the notion of perfection — pure academic bluff — in ferrying
      between tongues
is inconceivable, stupid and boring.

Think of a clown you love, a poor one of pathos and grace.

Carriage him to the next village over the frontier.
Translate his outfit, dress him in Hamlet's cape,
give him a target of ghosts and old claimants,
a gleaming foil and a gram of poison for the tip.

You'll hardly recognize how now the great actor, no fool,
leaps, laughs — a master fencer — and tumbles to applause.

Conceivable

Transfer Dwells in Imperfection

YES, translation of poetry is **conceivable.**
In a small room with desk and keyboard,
I am a verbal hood practicing the shameless art
of concealing an earlier author with a new passport,
a new language, and sharing a new voice for sale.

The transfer dwells in imperfection, the mother of freedom,

I shun mechanical replicas, the dream of literalists
(of older academics) who believe in absolute truth.
As a day worker I offer you a fresh and awakened other.
Out in the physical world the act of translation persists,
eternally cooking up likenesses and jumping genres.

We and the EARTH are forever translating ourselves.

Rain spills on carbon compounds (maybe once on MARS),
turning them into corn shoots and camellias.
Carcinoma's slow translation of the body kills.
Photosynthesis makes a life pact with the ubiquitous SUN,
the mother of translators. Over the millennia

SUN slowly converts ocean life into shouting cities.

Sun ink

Black Mind Translates World into Verse

About four billion years ago
a bang of atoms translated into constellations
   and dark energy. Our star
   rolls above us. Hot day rises
everywhere making love with icebergs and oceans.

   Pindar discovers that sun
cannot stop copulating with half our planet.
   Greek sungod Apollo glows
   rice paddies and snowfields.
Mirrored on the moon he drops romantically

   into nightclubs where he dances
as bonfire in our sweating bodies. Sun is creation.
   Sun is every artist's master
   translator, an unstoppable force
in the belly like sex for Goths who transcribe cities

   into rubble. Dark-souled
poet Georg Trakl of black wind and blue meadow
   hopes sun will freshen
   his suicidal landscape.
Sun converts his black words into fire of ink.

DIFFERENCE

SCARLET T OF TRANSLATION

Conversion is never exact and lives in **differences.**
In translation perfect mimesis is impossible.
      Difference is everywhere;
      breathe it in a foreign tongue.

Often the source is denied. But a fake or forgery
of earlier art is wonderful and not matricide.
      Brahms proudly cites Ludwig,
      Ravel revels in Mussorgsky,

Manet mimics Goya, Virgil thinks he is Homer.
In many eyes all imitation is museum shop replica
      of a Cycladic statue, a machine-
      made copy worth nothing.

But ancient glory is perplexing. In Bronze Age workshops
in the Cyclades they carve copies of copies of copies
      now priceless in museums
      of art and archeology

where curators of antiquity don't worry about simulacra,
nor Walter Benjamin's rage against mechanical reproduction.
      A translation (new reproduction)
      adds a fresh face of difference.

Masters Chaucer and Crashaw are candid forgers,
Yeats is not ashamed of his Byzantium goldsmith.
          But silly word cops arrest. Thugs
          bump off *Scarlet Letter* faces,

condemn the coupling of translator and author
as Trollopy, as whore work. A translation is
          a bastard child forced
          to wear a scarlet T around

her neck. We know who she is. A Yellow Star sewn
on a dress reveals a Jew's learned origin:
          Off to the camp! Knowledge
          of source brings her death.

Knowing past liaisons and adventures, Eve picks
forbidden fruit of gnosis from the garden tree
          She converts herself
          from obedient immortal

into the courageous mother of earthly heroes
who knows. For her gift she will die. Promethean Eve
          is the first artist to wear
          The Scarlet T of Translation.

20

Stained Knowledge

Counterfeits are Glorious

Forbidden apples and stained knowledge are a tasty tart.
    as counterfeits are glorious,
    a fake passport is classy.

The truly counterfeit translation hides its origin
    and masked aliens
    enters a new literature

as pseudepigrapha — false ascriptions — like authentic scriptures
    by the Buddha enough
    to fill a skyscraper,

like gospels of Markos, Mattityahu, and Yohannan,
    kid's song Frère Jacques,
    wartime "Lili Marleen"

and Shakespeare's *Romeo* transposed as Bernstein's
    West Side Story.
    As sinless natives

in written disguise, these old great works (invisibly
    different), can overthrow
    the avant-garde?

Exile

Exile, A Translation's Underworld Home

A translation dwells in **exile.** Do not ask it to return.
While its power derives from an earlier incarnation,
its existence in a new tongue should be inviolate,

immaculate, and demand total independence.
Beware of those who say translation is treachery.
They are **Inquisitors,** not lovers of the word,

Tea Party enforcers on the borderlands of art,
mocking the old word when it seeks a Green Card.
Exile is a translation's underworld home

yet the alien poem, reformed in another tongue,
may be different from anything ever sung before.
The Spanish mystic and poet Fray Luis de León

performs in his poems on an organ of the stars
and rises to an architecture of infinite song.
Down on earth the Augustinian monk gets five years

in the Inquisition Prison at Valladolid for Judaizing,
for rendering Song of Songs from the "corrupt original"
in Hebrew, not from the authorized Latin Vulgata.

Church Latin bullied its way to Bible ownership,
making both Greek and original Hebrew subversive.
With quiet magnificence Luis de León renders Horace and Job,

noting: *Poems in translation should not seem foreign
but born and natural in it* (nacidas en él y naturales).
Yet why not some flagrant unnaturalness?

Why not shake up English poetry with a young Rimbaud
who sees a minaret at the bottom of a well,
cathedrals in a lake and angels over pastures of emerald and steel?

Or the sudden arrogant figure of Mayakovsky
standing tall in his coalminer's cap,
shouting his syllables out to the sky from Brooklyn Bridge?

Why not the ghost of murdered Osip Mandelstamm
reading his alchemic lyrics about Stalin's moustache
or his exile poems from snows and his ice grave in Voronezh?

Lexical shock renews weary language bones.
A translation dwells in exile. It is good to drink
Turkish coffee in the pampas of the American Midwest.

FRIENDSHIP

YOUR SONG MAKES THE FRIENDSHIP BETWEEN POETS

Translation is **friendship** between two poets, an intimate union
that demands love, art and working with a foreign word.

Know François Villon's song in French
and the cello of his ballad will haunt you for life.

It is wondrous when you chat with a dead poet
in her own tongue, and return that grace with grace.

To return grace with grace is the aesthetic secret
of translation. Dictionaries help, but subvert if masters.

Know your author. Scholars are good servants of the text.
As translators beware. Spout Keats's cockney for a million years

but you won't bloom and die as young Jack Keats.
If you gossip in a lyric garden with a matchmaker

be wary of a human dictionary. Informants inform.
If pedantic they make chop meat of your tongue.

A graceless translator staggers in snow, freezes, and wins no seat
in the troika sled of poet, magical re-doer, and reader.

Young Robert Lowell laments:
Poems prepared by a taxidermist are likely to be stuffed birds.

FIDELITIES
FOREMOST TO BEAUTY

The poem floating on a forest brook is presumably
a wonder and worth the flow of vision and —
among authorial fidelities — foremost is **beauty.**
The translator paints the page with letters,
figures arise: some wind-blasting an oak at sunfall,
some tattooing rogue arms and legs with lilies.
The earthly artist has traduced our faith
if the new corpus lacks sex and beauty,
if the new book born of the old is not wet and worn
from so much eyesight and backpack road hiking,
if hungry asteroids, moons and blooming stars
don't touch the paper with commas and kisses.
When the perception of beauty does jump tongues,
a dancer on the rolling globe has holy grace.

GOOD

HARDCORE CROOKS AND SPINOZA

The Platonic **good** in the art of literature
is imitation and tradition and innovation.

All these *ions* are born in old blood.
Is there a great painter without a parent?

Scholars (I sneak in here) stick to annotated plagiarism,
a code word for admirable theft.

Translators are hardcore crooks. Unlike good literary
confidence men, their role is to get caught.

Among translators we have beautiful robbers.
Some dissemble — you might call our work fiction —

And some invent or combine or omit or improve
and behave like the two Roberts — Lowell and Bly.

It's healthy to declare freedom as the Roberts do.
Yet don't worry. The translation police

will not arrest you and pull out your tongue.
The best among us, Homer and Bible, swipe and are purloined,

wear facemasks and drift on through centuries undetected.
In Greek and Hebrew verse, the good author is a jewel thief

who smells the fire of ancestral poets and prophets
and dresses his verse with their glitter.

Baruch Spinoza, the prince of courageous originality,
the excommunicated Spanish-Portuguese Jew in the
    Amsterdam ghetto,

translates God into nature. His pantheistic world
is good and determined by reason.

Like Don Quijote de la Mancha (whose Castilian
is also the philosopher's native speech),

Baruch the lens grinder heretically fences with church
windmills. People say he is a living saint

and he discovers love everywhere. We live in it.
He tells us in Latin that our cosmos possesses all horizons.

In his ghetto refuge he roams from all the stars
back to a Portuguese olive grove of ancestral memory;

he controls the flight of a butterfly's singular day on earth,
whose few hours of being endure for an eternity.

LONDON

CHILDREN OF THE BIBLE

Consider the King JAMES VERSION.
All the finest rhetorical trickery went into its making.

Like the phoenix, the Bible's literary children
are reborn and change names and faces in disguise.

The huge progeny of the KJV
includes English speech and galaxies of poets,

major world poets called Solomon, David, Isaiah,
Jeremiah, Qoheleth of Ecclesiastes, Jesus of the Gospels,

and loquacious GOD on earth as the Voice in the Whirlwind
speaking to Moses and the Prophets

and arguing from the heavens with the poet Job.
None of these literary giants are in the Academy of Poets.

AUSTIN
HEBREW-GREEK BIBLE AS AN ENGLISH ORIGINAL

The Bible became an English original when in 1933
the **good** governor Ma Ferguson
holding up the King James Version proclaimed:

"If the King's English was good enough for Jesus Christ,
it's good enough for the children of Texas!"

Heaven

Preparing a Walk in Paradise

Translation is an instant of **Heaven.**

The poet in heat,

with skills and preparation for walking in **Paradise,**

remakes the **Earth.**

Independence

There Is No Original

A translation aspires to **independence.**
Even when achieved the dream is false.

Original work is neither independent nor original.

When the "original" is a handsome birth,
is its translation a secondary citizen?

Can Shakespeare's *Antony and Cleopatra*
surpass its ancient source in Plutarch?

Shakespeare's play dwarfs its thumbnail portrait.

Can the King James Version share the glory
of the canonical Hebrew Bible? Almost.

Ancient tests in a new tongue depend
on hand of translator and eyes of reader.

The secular creation of scripture is the last of a string
of Buddhist rebirths and transformations.

Like time scripture starts long ago. It has
no beginning and so no originality.

A translation is a first acknowledgment of a string
of original rebirths involving two artists who remake each other.

All literature is translation from a tradition;
all translation is a unique instant of shared tradition

and perfectly original. Genealogy is fun and futile.

Original & Translation
Each Text Unique Yet An Earlier Voice

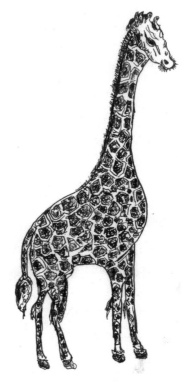

Octavio Paz, arranging continents like a giraffe
who sees over treetops, declares: *Every text is unique
and at the same time is a translation of an earlier voice.*

O & T, the formula for **Original** & **Translation,**
gives us: $O = T = O = T$ from now to eternity.
This formula of infinite exchange of attributes

offers licentious innovation to praise or abuse
or, packing your word-gun, to possess the text with impunity.
If you hover between **O** & **T** and find no word to describe

your chair in nowhere, you may be wise as well
as wordless. To run out of words is **Illumination**
and is a proper lexical starvation for poet, diplomat,

philosopher, and the night vision owl who can only see far.

IMITATION & INTERPRETATION
PERFECT PINKIES OF A SAFECRACKER

The charged words "imitation" and "interpretation"
taste of honey from the Midi or swell with verbal venom.

You may be praised as part of the great tradition
of Boccaccio, Chaucer and Yeats, the super re-doers,

or slammed in place as a COPYCAT.
A new version may be commended

as an independent original born outside the universe,
or reviled as an ignoble translation weary of time

or delicious like the dinner of the ambling crane
who translates worms into intestinal pleasure.

Our imperfect epithet for the fine translator is
Imitator, Smuggler, Tinker, Thief & Spy.

Lastly, a *redemptive* translator is a musician
Who interprets notes on a staff into sound.

like Catalan Pablo Casals mellowing his "Song of the Birds"
or Dame Myra Hess fingering Brahms's chaste thunder

or Andrés Segovia plucking Plato's sonorous cowbells.
Musicians look at ink and listen to sound.

They leap over a concert hall ceiling
until dangling alone in the eardrum of space,

employ both their mouth and fingers
to play like Apollo with sunbeams.

A fine musician translates the score
with the perfect pinkies of a safecracker.

Morocco

Kisses Recalled Through Interpretive Melody

War year 1942, lonely and let down,
sitting on his Casablanca bar stool,
tough guy Humphrey Bogart looks to Sam, his song interpreter,
for comfort.
Nazi Major Strasser will soon storm into his café,
Ingrid Bergman of Paris days will soon escape by morning plane.
Bogart and Ingrid want earlier kisses and love back again
through an **interpretive** melody.
Sam at piano has the singing translator's fingers and voice
to re-create old times. Ingrid is desolate.
Lonely Ingrid remembering, feeling old times
and the soulful key tune to past sighs and glory,
pushes the piano player to play it again:
Play it, Sam. Play "As Time Goes By."

JOKE

A THOUSAND EARLIER MOTHERS

A good translation is a good **joke.** Reader, you're fooled.
The transformed word has no beginning
and it is madness to look for an *OED* original.
Good or bad, beauty or trash, ancient or today,
a **joke** lurks under the text. Read a line
and discover a thousand earlier mothers.
Since the dream of capturing and freezing words
is an iceberg, an allegory for death, a bad joke,
it is best to greet change and impermanence
and the impossibility of cloning Plato
or testing translation with bottom-of-page placebos.
If you're tired of the readymade, spend a day of change
with peppy Proteus and elevator man Heraclitus.
These two Greek **jokers** will rock you into sublimity.

KABBALAH

TRANSLATORS COMPETING WITH THE CREATOR

Translation aspires to **Kabbalah**
wherein the universe is lawful though fiery words
yet wakes down on earth to the knowledge
of instability and impermanence.

Can we ask miracles from human translators
to grace us with a poem? Absolutely.
The poet translator competes with the Creator
who has converted himself into being and divinity.

In ignorance we translate windy chaos into illumination,
better and more veracious than afterlife.
My preference cult is the eternal Gnostic singing
found in the *Coptic Manichaean Songbook.*

Kabbalists and Spanish mystics and Gnostics
and translators all share a conspiracy of dissent,
to make the poem live alone in an unknown tongue
and radiate integrity for a monolingual reader.

The poem has no hope of becoming an Olympic star
until the translator shapes it into formal light.
That light is heard as the call in the ancient deserts
and the Kabbalists read the beams on alphabet leaves

hanging from a wisdom tree. The beams are ineffable,
yet their ecstatic sound is deciphered as a poem.
Like a performing singer the song is erect like a lion

gleaming authority, and incised on the Pharaoh's tomb wall.

Zohar וֹהַר

Translation Moves into the Light

In the *Zohar Book of Radiance* the *eyn sof*
Lies not in black solidity.

Within the concealed mind cave
a black flame issues from the mystery of *eyn sof*,

becomes a fog forming in the unformed
and springs forth into luminosity.

From that tree of light,
Adam sees from one end to the other of the world

like the eternal gazelle of hill and savanna
to reveal original mystery to the world.

His eyes translate darkness into a bright book
of the architecture of black atoms, of green cries

on sexual meadows, and a basket of stars.

مولانا بلال الـدين مهمد دوص

RUMI A BIRD OF LIGHT

In 1207 Jalal al-Din **Rumi**
is born at Balkh near the Afghan frontier.
    He will die in Konia in Byzantine
    Rum after a life of seeking —
like 30 pilgrims — the mystical bird.

    Only with that bird will he
have power to transform the world. His friend
    comes at night, tells him
    to eat with his mouth closed.
He hungers, examines the cross, a Hindu

    temple, an ancient pagoda,
and finds no trace of the bird. He climbs
    the mountain of Kaf. Even
    in Mecca there are no wings.
He asks the philosopher Avicena. No word.

    Rumi translates day to night,
life to death, sun to rock, and seeks any way
    of converting random love
    into a source on meadows,
or heaven, even under the desert rocks. As for

human lovers, with whom
he learns the science of ecstasy, he feels empty
        and turns his back on them.
        With no bird of light
he is impotent. The Sufi poet moves thought

        into slow night and opens
his eyes to dark. Yet as a hermit he scarcely
        moves. Without light
        he loses hope of translating
the world. His hands hang like lifeless coins

        in sagging pockets and he
and the world jam to a halt. Jalal al-Din Rumi
        seems dead, but memory
        has not ceased. He recalls
how as a child along the Afghan border with China

        he witnesses great herds of herons
and flamingos filling the horizon and suddenly
        swooping onto the sand
        where with literary alchemy
they leave the infinite alphabet of white peace.

        Landing on one foot, their claws
turn into fire and melted crystal sand into broken
        Chinese ink spelling
        an undeciphered ecology
of Asia. The Sufi poet rambles through all fresh

words in the cosmos. He
must carry into Persian verse interior clouds,
     butcher shops and the gardens.
     There remains a single droplet
of low flame in his eyes. In that stillness Rumi

     is staring, a disturbed creator,
yet he perceives sparks moving out of black clouds,

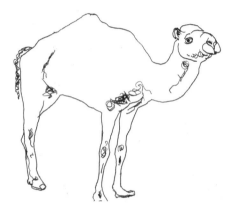

     camels with lakes below
     their humps, pheasant tracks
that print Chinese calligraphy on earth. Floods

     drown Mesopotamia dotted
with ravens, ibises and underworlds. Yet how
     can he transfer the cosmos
     to visible ink? Rayless within,
his ink is black on black, his eyes looking

     inward are totally blank.
Rumi turns his head down and sees where he
     hasn't gone. Through mist of
     vague brain sparks of nowhere
he glares at a **bird of light** dancing in his lungs.

LETTER

KABBALISTS ADORE WHIMSY AND
SWINGING LETTERS

Religion is God's bureaucracy
and fidelity to a word gathers as holy script.

Grave obedience to a phrase
issues crystalline faith no sledgehammer splits.

However, Kabbalists play and adore whimsy.
                    Their swinging letters are ciphers.
In old drawings a tree of life has leaves as letter numbers

and a man's body covered at vital spots
with the ten virtue letters of the Sefirot.
                    on satin of white fire lying on God's lap.

After God creates the world with words,
he engraves his twenty-two letters of the alphabet
on stone and parchment with his pen of flame.

He composes holy Torah with black fire.
In one flash he draws Eden, Eve and Adam in Paradise
                                        where

among Fowls of the air,

Plodders on the earth,

Fishes wiggling in waters

there is no knowledge and no wrong.

Adam the namer of every Garden dweller
chooses a single letter to mark each beast
with letters for their heart and grand nimbleness.

He translates them into tribes:

Obedient oxen in the meadow   Peaceful dove in the sun

Voyage mule on the hill

Savvy serpent on the ginko tree

Feeder cows by the house   Tiny fishes in the rivers

and Mammoth elephants in Ethiopia

for roaming the Wild or lingering in a Zoo

all awaiting Eve to tattoo them with knowledge
of temporal honeymoon on earth.

Elephant
Lumbering Literalists

The Elephant is ponderous in step. His memory is nimble
and once he smells you as a friend you are never more
in danger. He has trouble dancing on a thimble
but birds adorn and clean his leather coat so he can soar

in thought of mighty copulation. Hence his herd
will grow and he will howl with pleasure and vast thunder
as he translates his sperm into daughter or son.
Wisest of beasts the elephant can't bear the blunder

of literalists. Like hunters they seek ivory, not his sun
or moonlight walks. When evil hunters come, his birds
alert him with a friendly trill. He pulls a tree up with his trunk.
Before a trigger clicks, he's got the poachers on the run.

Before murderers, the elephant trumpets lyric words
to friendly buffalo and wildebeest and pounds a hunk
of forest on the hunter's bean. Thrilled, the savannah leaps
and twitters every malignant poacher: *Be gone for keeps!*

LITERALISM
HORACE AND JEROME ABHOR LITERALISM

Both Horace and Jerome draw back from **literalism**
of word-for-word to champion phrase and sense,
and whatever miracle they choose to shape Latin, Greek
and Hebrew, be it Kabbalah letters hanging on a tree
or sunset rising in Ecclesiastes, eclectic Horace
and Jerome are safe and free. They will not be struck down.
Their poem, even locked in the Prophets' *Moby Dick* prose
or in marble Latin meters of outrageous Eros,
is forever delicious and sensually read and reread.

Master

Shaping Old Clay into a New Vessel

An artist translator is a **master** potter.
The potter is given the content of spirit
from an old pot and a recollection of its shape.

*

Mastery lies in manipulating the clay into a new pot.
Then in her own distinct language
she pours content into a form of her own creation.

*

The translator is the Chinese ceramicist
who recreates the spirit and makes and shapes
the new vessel in which that spirit lives.

Nothingness

From Nada Comes Todo

The translator plays with **nothingness,**
De nada a todo, from nothing to all.

Saint John of the Cross inserts *De nada a todo*
into a concrete poem drawing:

        nada
        nada
        nada
        nada
        nada
        nada
        nada
        nada
        nada
        ¡todo!

In *nada* the Spanish poet saint finds his all.
In his erotic *Cántico espiritual* the lovers

in a black night of the soul
go with only sun in the heart guiding them

to the sonorous silence of ineffable love.
In John's untranslatable verse

dwells a fertile meadow of translation
and the best wild herbs on the horizon.

De nada a todo. De nada a todo.

OUT OF BABEL
BRIGHT FACES FROM ANCIENT RUINS

What has never been done in the target language
expands thematic and formal boundaries

and brightens literature for both monolingual readers
and writers seeking to grow idea and art.

Traditions of theme and form are altered
by infusions of poems from other lands,

especially from quick energy and impossible babbling
heard in new tongues bequeathed by **Babel.**

Ocean

Translatio: Big Mover of the Seas

The art of *translatio* consists of carting words across.
Translation is voyage and the poet boards a translation

to cross the **ocean.** Any ship of any description
may be qualified to reach port, sailing across

the "Sea of Fidelity" or the "Sea of License."

The port too will suggest in its name the conditions
of the sea by which the ship reaches its destination.
So the port where the cargo of poems lies anchored may be called

"Saint Faithful" or "New Harmony" or "Wild Strawberries."

But the port must have a jargony abstract name.
Hero Charles Baudelaire earned his living translating
the complete short stories of Edgar Allan Poe into French.

For your Baudelarian "l'Invitation au Voyage"
choose one of the essential names for your carrier ship:

> After
> Conversion
> Interlingalism
> Intralingualism
> Imitation
> Other Voice
> Metaphrase
> Paraphrase
> Recreation
> Restoration
> Retelling
> Second Birth
> Transference
> Transformation
> Translation
> Treachery
> Version

In actual practice of the art, tip your cards to the reader.

The ocean of a thousand sounding tongues and ports tells
a thousand ways of translating your journey to them.
Any craft may lead to the chosen port, but name the ship.

ORCHARDS OF THE FRUIT
WAKING ANCIENT GREEK FIGS

Now, moving from the ocean inland up to the **orchards,**
if we endow the trees and their fruit with proper names,
we hungry readers and critics should eat well.

Re-waken Sappho on a hilly field on a Greek island
of wrestling olive trees guarding the gold wheat
under that rational light of the Mediterranean.

Save her candor of mind and body, her metric genius,
whose abundant perfect lyrics — Plato's "tenth muse" —
were burnt by command of popes and patriarchs.

Seven centuries before the common era
Archilochos writes about figs and wanton women
and his own wild shameless military orgies:

"Weary are the muscles in my mushroom."
The poems of this earliest poet of the lyre,
with terrible midnight sun burning him

as the "Paros Dog Star of Eros,"
have been modernized as mere fragments.
Holy church translator axmen chop up the papyri

and parchments of Archilochos's pagan codices
or gesso them over for inscribing monastery hymnals;
worst is weather and time translating ink into dust.

Yet the art of translation has wonderfully carted
some fruit from his island orchard over the water
and we have a taste of sergeant commander Archilochos

and imagine multiple trees in a Greek patch
of green terraces sleeping on the afternoon hill
below fatal sun still in watermelon heavens.

He is there in the fullness of the sonorous silence
of a thousand poems that have disappeared.
Loss of writings by great artists is a melancholy

translation of genius into absence. The early death
of Apollinaire, Lorca, Dylan Thomas, Gershwin,
Modigliani, Van Gogh, Mozart is transformation of brain

into an infinity of otherness, into ugly eternity
that somehow enhances their surviving wonders
that we love. And then we pause and desire more.

Gardener, the Re-Creator
Peaches in New Garments

The **gardener** has opened the way into the orchard
for you to pick and consume.
She may have decided to turn a peach tree into a prickly pear.
She has all kinds of phonic and cultural excuses
for making word-things switch meaning.

The gardener may think you are looking at her own body
and hides behind her new garments of beauty.
If you see her naked in the faithful raw,
you may not look long.
Once you decide to eat from her orchard,
if you eat a prickly pear for a peach,
be fair to her, the art maker, and don't make ugly faces.

Enjoy.

Punishment

Err and Go Straight to Jail

The right comeuppance for a **mistake** is capital **punishment.**

Freedom to invent, stray from the text,
even to FBI black-out whole passages
is all perfectly okay if you confess by naming what you do
or don't confess but joy us back to an older author's face.

But freedom of error?
That crime puts a writer on the hot seat.
Only a double-crossing punk sees freedom and error as twins.

Yet if you are wrong, even if flagrantly mistaken,
go easy. You're human. Truce! You may be Icarus

misreading the sun, Yeats dining with Madame Blavatsky.
Even the fabled jackal, a pal of Pharaohs,

misreads a twilight leopard for a lamb.
The sky fox of Africa is **punished** as feline supper.

To err is human, but at breakfast,

please don't put salt in the sugar bowl
or orange juice on oatmeal. Bon appétit.

QUINTILIAN

WRITER'S SKILLS SHARPENED BY TRANSLATION

The writer's skills, as **Quintilian** pompously knows,
are increased by exercising the act of translation.
Of course Quintilian, being an eloquent grammarian,
suggests the translation of **prose** oration, not the **poem.**
Quintilian rules the day, and those riffraff poets,
Catullus and his student Juvenal sing immoderately
unlike the theory master of figurative speech and tropes.
The Latin grammarians and orators have trouble
with shady poets who cannot invent a murder plot
to kill an emperor or at least maim a senile senator.
Though as a rhetorician Quintilian champions translation,
he tends to **Q** the wandering lyric scum behind the **8-ball.**

Robber

Confess Your Crime and Look for Praise

T. S. Eliot likes to shock with his truths:
Minor poets borrow, major poets steal.
Like every writer the translator robs the past,
or, more politely, leans on tradition.
But the translator has a special contract
with an earlier voice. Both names are on the title page.

It is good to hear the early voice. If it is song
from 13-century Troubadours in Provence
or street madrigals in Elizabethan London
the hour is rhyme. Let old song be overheard.
Edward Fitzgerald gave us Omar Khayyam,
sugaring a mathematician's mystical quatrains.

I wish Robert Frost, Elizabeth Bishop or Richard Wilbur
would plunder Omar, openly or by sleuth,
and peal the Persian Sufi's meditations in a long poem.

If murder and complete **robbery** are necessary, be open.
It may be an admirable and praised crime

like the labor of hyenas who clean up the mess of nature,
those unglamorous garbage men of death
who translate corpses into chunks of vitamins.

The crime may be of a strictly formal composer
who translates wayward lovers into tragic song
and whose night howl is Pavarotti at La Scala.

STRICTURES

WRITING WITH LIGHT ON A SONOROUS PAGE

The skill of a translator poet is tested by **strictures.**
There is as much freedom in a close version

as in a free one. English syntax is boundless
and likes to be challenged to change its ways,

welcoming writers who imaginatively abuse.
A close rendering requires mountaintop imagination.

If you fall, so what? The real DANGER is seduction
by the word-for-word facile surface of literality.

The paradox: To be close and nimble and free
vault twenty times to cross the bar once,

or leap like Thomas Traherne over the moon.
In close translation you can soar above the clouds

to compensate for clogging up the planet.
To be close to mystery sounds, hug the sky.

The translator poet wears a good space suit,
has extraordinary fingers for directing flight.

But enter sloth and expect to splash like a hippo in a river.
Close or far in meaning may or may not work

but if you seek formal regularity in prosody, *en garde!*
Classical verse can beat you up unless you are

the genius humpback Alexander Pope.
Keeping heroic couplets in painful constraint,

Pope cleans up Shakespeare's plays (ouch) and lays them straight.
He is translator of his age, adored by Samuel Johnson

and by Robert Fitzgerald our own master,
but modest Fitzgerald roars out of Greek dactyls

into loose pentameters intimately agile with sense.
He writes with light across a sounding page.

On Homer's Sea

The Five-Beat Prance   Robert Fitzgerald (1910–85)

Sometimes Fitz works for weeks for a few lines.
Irishman from Illinois he plays with Greek epic
in Italy and in a house on Homer's sea where winter
storms bash the rocks below in noisy metrics.
He docs his first translation at Harvard
of an ode by Horace he doesn't care for
to soothe financial **strictures.** He needs the 200-
buck prize money; doesn't win it. Then keeps
to a five-beat prance in Homer and Virgil till one
can hear their sixes. All that discipline for the ear
helped the earliest singers to remember.
From Troy and Carthage back to Sicily
Fitz swims easy five-stroking the grape sea.
In describing the way of great Tang poets
the Chinese say they are *dancing in chains.*

Translatio to a Second Birth

The Grand Movers

A translating poet must be a translator poet with an ABC degree in the art of *translatio*.

In rendering poetry from nothing into something, the translator poet works for wondrous new breath, even during the religion wars and he is William Tyndale (1492–1536) in prison near Brussels awaiting strangulation and fire on the pyre for his for-the-ploughboy version of the New Testament, not rendered from the authorized Vulgata but directly from the original Greek.

For poetic mastery in the final English version, if she is Mary Herbert or Catullus or Elizabeth Bishop or Boris Pasternak, we will be amazingly lucky, but as Octavio Paz says: "Even good poets need to learn the art of 'the other voice.'"

Critical is when the poem jumps tongues in that second of conversion-truth when fire and knowledge commingle to create art.

In that "second birth," in that flashing instant, the poem becomes everything or nothing.

BLACK MOON OF DEATH
CRY OF THE ECLIPSE

After August 18th, 1936, when Federico García Lorca, hand-cuffed to an anarchist bullfighter and a Republican school-teacher, falls to the bullets of the Black Squad near Ainadamar, "The Fountain of Tears," his literary voice abroad depends on translators, who in giving him speech are poets who also master the art of being interlingual carriers of song; who experience the second of conversion.

Through the new song Lorca's black moon, the cry of eclipse from valley to valley, his boy eating oranges on a balcony, or dead man lying in the street whose open eyes once can no can no longer look into, come alive in every tongue.

Unknown

Stumble in the Unknown and See Light

A translator operates in the **unwise** and the **unknown**
and gambles on gains to balance her losses.

Clichés in the original often freshen in the new tongue.
Be courageous. Give a cliché new life,

say it. Don't fudge. Don't take a poll. That's not the way
of lonely artists. Utter the exotic.

Report the words of the sober Maya god Copac
about to drink a jug of royal hot chocolate.

Indulge in literal translation of a worn cliché
and it will shine like an old silver dime.

Safe equivalents cause pain and demean.
All around you in the obvious stands the **unknown**.

Antony

Choosing Beauty Before His
Translation into Shade

Shakespeare waltzes his exalted Alexandrian play
of Antony and Cleopatra right out of a thumbnail
version in Plutarch's *Parallel Lives*. The theft is silken.
Cavafy also raids Plutarch. Hooray for larceny.
Constantine Cavafy of Alexandria poignantly has Antony
go to the window to hear the mysterious troupe
of musicians passing below in the streets of Alexandria.
A roar from the city gates, the gods abandon Antony.
Not as a whining coward but as one graced with courage
Antony goes firmly to the window and listens
with deep emotion to the voices, to the exquisite music
of that strange invisible procession
and says goodbye to her, to the Alexandria he is losing,
before his last step, before he falls on his sword.

VIRTUE

CONVERTING TALK INTO GREEK & WORLD SCRIPTS

Socrates chats and Plato overhears
and converts talk into the *Dialogues*.

Plato plays the modest scribe
to preserve the philosophic back and forth
and spontaneity of the great Greek speaker.

Socrates gives up his life (a frightening act) to save
the integrity of an idea.

His thought and life Plato turns into permanence.
Their chatter sneaks into the world's scripts
where it lingers as a memory forever in our lungs.

Translation of thought and actions within a language
is an intralingual summit.

Plato's conversion is peak **virtue.**

WRITER

AGAINST ARCHAISM

The translator is a **writer** with arguments against archaisms,
who talks modern but not so fearfully as to rub out the past.

Old writers will not lose the quality of their age
when heard in contemporary diction.

Remember, in the speech of their day
the writer was not archaic but perfectly modern.

Forget everything stilted. Be verbally just and fresh
as a Cycladic island dish of tomatoes and cucumbers.

Unless you are Edmund Spenser on an archaic kick,
creating a medieval Fairie Queene with dragons and knights

for your welcoming Tudor patron Queen Elizabeth,
beware of silly old talk. If you must be a throwback,

good luck and count on nothing.

X-RAY

THROUGH A PAGE TO ANOTHER LAND

A translation is an **X-Ray,** not a Xerox.

A poet translator is a **xenophile**
who hears Marco Polo's rivers in Xanadu,
a damsel playing her dulcimer on Mount Abora;

sees marble palaces, fierce gyrfalcons, pet leopards,
and Kubla Khan's X-rated nights in Mongolia.

A literary X marks the hot spot
on the tropical coast of huapango Mexico

where fishing occurs at sea and in a Vera Cruz bed,
where virginity converts to adulthood,

where huge white flowers dance to a booming xylophone.

Yhwh's ABC of Creation

Through Adam's Mouth

Our Mesopotamian God Yahweh is the first translator.
He will declare the light
and light will be his drawing pen for live pictures.
But before he calls the cosmos into being,
he needs to possess letters and words
to separate the light from the darkness,
and the waters of heaven from the waters of the earth.

His letters he makes out of black fire placed on velvet
and with two words he translates chaos into galaxies,
the sun and moon, the firmaments and us.
When creating animals and naming them through
the mouth of Adam, he decides to vary his equine creatures.
When translating Asian horse into African zebra

YHWH adds stripes rather than spots

so Adam won't think his **Z-beast** a leopard.

God and Adam share the tasks of creation:
God the magician, Adam the namer of names,
and to keep the world fascinated
God transforms a stubborn windowpane-pecking white wren
into a laughing percussionist named Isaac, meaning laughter,

adding relentless rap and jazz rhythm to the act of translation.

LET THERE BE LIGHT
יְהִי אוֹר (YEHI OR)

We are created before we read. After creation
come Bible makers with Torah ink to record
how Yahweh with two black words יְהִי אוֹר
commands light into chaos to replace darkness,
how he **translates** his solitude into worlds,
how he transports his children like clouds
onto precincts of multiple lands and the firmament
of cows, eagles and angels, and how at death
he drops us to burn in the garbage pit of Gehenna.
God is World Translator and master poker player
with an invisible Ace of Hearts to transform spirit.
The Creator shines stage light on earthly translation.

ALEPH ALPHA ALIF IS DREAM
THE ABC OF IGNORANCE

Aleph calls on us to love the universal babble
and chaos on holy temple streets. We hear sounds

of impenetrable prayer and beautiful song
from **Aleph** to **Tav** in crypts deep below Toledo.

We hear hymns from **Alpha** to **Omega** composed
by daring Byzantine abbess Kassia in Contantinople.

In the Mosque of Omar in Jerusalem we hear
chanted Qur'an from **Alif** to **Ta** rise to Jannah Paradise.

We hapless listeners are searching for a sweet fix
from unknown sacerdotal song composed in

Aleph   Beth   Gimel

Alpha   Beta   Gamma

Alif   Ba   Ta

Though ignorant of their sense, we dream
of **translating** the Creator's words into a guide

to a year or a day more of life on this globe
below our beautiful but fatal Ecclesiastes sun.

Y U?

HERE'S TO U, READER

A translator spends a life asking **Y**?

yet this mortal **I**,
even puffed up as a seeing-I

dog guide, knows my wandering gypsy **Y**
is a deep longing for **U**.

So I head out on streets of the world and **J**-walk,
hop over metered lines on **B** meadows,

to carry **G**-wizz my astonished **O** over to **U**.

ZOHAR

BOOK OF SPLENDOR

Good translation is essential to a hungry reader
in a decent bookstore in our global village. We are in need.
        We still work under Yahweh's
                edict of expulsion

from the monolingual Tower of Babel
that gave us a diaspora of many tongues
        and the dragoman interpreter
                of multilingual babble

heard in caravans roaming along the Silk Road.
Translation is a Chinese **Zen** (禅) metaphor
        for an unknown zero
                equaling the burning zenith.

Translation plays with chaos, infusing a mass
with colors as radiant as the Spanish **Zohar.**
        Translation is **wrongly**
                a modest profession,

and suffers, *mamma mía,* shame and confusion,
yet each recreation of SPLENDOR makes new poets:
        those who craft the light
                and those who hear.

Want to read a poem deeply? Translate it.
Want to be a poet? Translate a volume of poems.
If translation is your sun,
you are a savior

like Pico della Mirandola who lived and died
to bring unknown Zohar into a gracious light.
Translation dreams of being
a *Book of Splendor.*

BLACK NIGHT
A MYSTICAL POET

On a dark night in August,
1587, the Spanish mystical poet
      Juan de la Cruz, a silk merchant's
      son born Juan Yepes, lies on
a cot in a dungeon closet for nine months

      in the Carmelite Monastery
in Toledo except for Friday evenings
      when he's taken out to be
      bullwhipped on his back
by a circle of the brothers. He babbles,

      afflicted with love, and in
his astonished babble loses sense as he
      converts oblivion into a theater
      of vision. There, in darkness of
his soul he sees the woman of the Song of Songs

and transfers her to a street
in the city where no one seems to be.
They walk to the country,
lie together under the wind
by the castle wall, and the wind wounds

their napes in ecstasy. Sun
shines in their hearts, more friendly than
the dawn. Juan de la Cruz
is the ultimate translator.
He converts babble into silent flight,

biblical verse and his dungeon
cot into woman, a countryside romp into
wounding winds, night
into noon, and the aridity
of his soul into a country bed of love

by oblivious lilies in efficient
transforming dream. The mystical poet
carries that vision with him
when he ties together a rope
made from torn sheets, slips from his window

down a steep wall to the court-
yard, and then tiny Juan with help from
la Virgin hops over the steep
outer wall of the monastery.
On a black night, inflamed by love, he escapes.

Next morning in a convent
of his discalced sisters, Juan, good at miracles
of composition, translates his
soul's dark night to a canticle of love
he comes on randomly while catching his **Zs.**

Cuckoo
Converting the Globe

The **cuckoo** is a bird   whose bell is heard
when her name is said.   Then a bell of lead
becomes a sphere   of silver to the ear
and every tree   blooms like a dappled sea
of fruit and mist,   and every hill is kissed
with **cuckoo cuckoo**   echo echo too
beautiful for song.   The **cuckoo** is not for long
in his love nest,   but lays his eggs to rest
each night with a   new love, then flits away.
I am surprised and pleased   to hear her seized
with tricks, content   on the first continent
with her own flock   of thorn trees. Soon I'll dock
far from her thorn   trees here. I'm nor forlorn.
as stars appear   never can she disappear
or cease her **cuckoo** note   making me float.

91

FORMED BY THE ANCIENTS
READING TRANSLATIONS OF ANTIQUITY

How beautiful to read the Greek
and Roman thinkers. They compose
the good with reason and a tweak
of wild epiphany in prose
and metric song. Epicurus
stoically into atoms and
a peaceable being declares shush
to death. I wear a wedding band
reading in gold: *Do not forget
the ancients.* They are our breakfast.
They have the wisdom and we too
brood on living forever. Set
a Plato dish for us, for you,
for inner sun so we will last.

ABC of Beasts

The Nightingale Transports Ecstasy

The nightingale's keen specialty
is translating her ecstasy.

The spider spins a harplike cage
of silence echoing John Cage.

The lazy **lion** yawns and soars
transforming sloth into her roar.

Dante translate his lovers in-
to icy Hell for carnal sin.

The Spanish mystic wakes to sleep,
transporting light for his deep leap.

Blake's chimney sweepers in soot flues
turn dead and we hear children's blues.

A newborn's cry is her transfer
of need and wonder to her mère.

Beasts are translators in our ear
waking black moons to help us hear

how poets play from unknown tongues
an ABC of Solomon's songs.

NOTES

The epigrams in "On Translation" are from Edwin Honig's *The Poet's Other Voice: Conversations on Literary Translation.* Amherst: University of Massachusetts Press, 1985.

In **E** Luis de León's words are from the *Apologia* to his poems. For more on Fray Luis de León, see my *The Unknown Light: The Poems of Fray Luis de León,* State University Press of New York, 1976.

In **F** Robert Lowell's comment is from *Imitations.* New York: The Noonday Press, 1965.

In **L** Octavio Paz's words are from *Traducción: Literatura y literalidad.* 1971. rpt: Barcelona: Tusquets Editores, 1981.

In **K, L,** and elsewhere, references to Kabbalah (קבלה) from Gershom Scholem, Ed., Zohar, New York: Schocken Books, 1963; Mario Satz, *Umbría lumbre: San Juan de la Cruz y la sabiduría secreta en la Kábala y el Sufismo.* Madrid: Hiperión, 1991; and my *The Other Bible: Jewish Pseudepigrapha, Christian Apocypha, Gnostic Scriptures, Kabbalah, Dead Sea Scrolls.* Harper & Row, San Francisco, 1984.

In Kabbalah, Zohar in Aramaic רהז, meaning "radiance" or "splendor," is a collection of Aramaic commentaries on the Torah, attributed to Moisés de León (1250?–1305) in Spain, who himself ascribes the volume to Shimon Yochai, a second-century Talmudic commentator. However, Gershom Sholem, on the basis of Aramaic syntax and the inclusion of Spanish phrases (transcribed into the Hebrew alphabet), establishes the work as a thirteenth-century composition.

Zohar was a primary source for the essential mystical writings of the rabbinical Spanish scholar Isaac Luria (1534–1572), who spread Kabbalah to communities in Italy, Egypt, and Israel, which has been called Lurianic Kabbalah.

Jalal al-Din Rumi, in Farsi (Persian) is usually known by his complete name, مولانا بـلالل الـدين محمد دوص, Mawlana Jalal al-Din Muhammad Rumi.

In **N** the Spanish words *De nada a todo* means *From nothing to everything*. Here and in Zen, Saint John of the Cross (1542–1591), in Spanish San Juan de la Cruz, the great Spanish mystical poet. John's *Cántico espiritual* (Spiritual Canticle) is derived in his way from the biblical Song of Songs. See my *The Poems of Saint John of the Cross*, New Directions, 1973.

In Zohar zen is the Japanese pronunciation of a Sino-Japanese character 禅, pronounced *chan* in Mandarin, referring to Chan Buddhism which traditionally entered China in the sixth century C.E, from India; *chan* derives from Sanskrit *dhyana* and Pali *jhana*.

In Zohar the subtitle "Black night" refers to *Noche oscura del alma*, "Dark Night of the Soul" by Juan de la Cruz (St John of the Cross). In it Juan speaks in the female voice of the Shulamite woman who finds her invisible lover prince and loses self in physical union with him. His source is the Latin translation of the השירים שיר, *shir ha-shirim,* the biblical Song of Songs. So Juan's poem goes from Hebrew to Greek to Latin to his Spanish re-creation of the mystical experience rendered, like the ultimate Hebrew source, in secular diction.

In YHWH, יהוה, is the Tetragrammaton, Greek for "word with four letters," and one of the ineffable names of God, though it is usually pronounced as Adonai, meaning lord. In modern translations YHWH is transcribed as Yahweh; in earlier biblical versions, such as the Tyndale and King James Version, Yahweh is Jehovah.

"Be light" is from יְהִי אוֹר, *yehi or,* normally rendered, "Let there be light."

א, alef or aleph, is the first letter and ת, tav, is the last letter of the Hebrew alphabet. The set of the first three letters of the alphabet are: Hebrew Aleph, Beth, Gimel; Greek Alpha, Beta, Gamma; and Arabic Alif, Ba, Ta.

INDEX OF NAMES AND CONCEPTS

BOOKS BY WILLIS BARNSTONE

POETRY

Poems of Exchange
From This White Island
Antijournal
A Day in the Country
New Faces of China
China Poems
Overheard
A Snow Salmon Reached the Andes Lake
Ten Gospels and a Nightingale
The Alphabet of Night
Five A.M. in Beijing
Funny Ways of Staying Alive
The Secret Reader • 501 Sonnets
Algebra of Night: New & Selected Poems (1948–1998)
Life Watch
Café de l'Aube
Stickball on 88th Street

TRANSLATIONS

Eighty Poems of Antonio Machado. Introduction by John
    Dos Passos; Reminiscence by Juan Ramón Jiménez.
The Other Alexander: Greek novel by Margarita Liberaki
    (with Helle Barnstone)
Greek Lyric Poetry

Physiologus Theobaldi Episcopi (Bishop Theobald's Bestiary)
Sappho: Poems in the Original Greek with a Translation
The Poems of Saint John of the Cross
The Song of Songs
The Poems of Mao Zedong
My Voice Because of You: Pedro Salinas. Preface by Jorge
    Guillén
The Unknown Light: Poems of Fray Luis de León
A Bird of Paper: Poems of Vicente Aleixandre. Preface by
    Vicente Aleixandre (with David Garrison)
Laughing Lost in the Mountains: Poems of Wang Wei
    (with Tony Barnstone and Xu Haixin)
Six Masters of the Spanish Sonnet: Quevedo, Sor Juana Inés
    de la Cruz, Machado, Lorca, Borges, Miguel Hernández
To Touch the Sky, 1998: Poems of Mystical, Spiritual and
    Metaphysical Light
Sonnets to Orpheus by Rainer Maria Rilke
Border of a Dream: Selected Poems of Antonio Machado
Sweetbitter Love: Poems by Sappho
Ancient Greek Lyrics
Love Poems of Pedro Salinas and Katherine Letter Poems

MEMOIR

With Borges on an Ordinary Evening in Buenos Aires
Sunday Morning in Fascist Spain: A European Memoir
    (1948–1953)
We Jews and Blacks: Memoir with Poems (with Yusef
    Komunyakaa)

LITERARY CRITICISM

The Poetics of Ecstasy: From Sappho to Borges
The Poetics of Translation: History, Theory, Practice
ABC of Translation

BIBLICAL

The Other Bible: Intertestamental Scripture
Apocalypse (Book of Revelation)
The New Covenant : Four Gospels and Apocalypse
The Restored New Testament, Including the Gnostic
    Gospels of Thomas, Mary, and Judas
The Gnostic Bible (with Marvin Meyer)
Essential Gnostic Scriptures (with Marvin Meyer)
Masterpieces of Gnostic Wisdom: CD (with Marvin Meyer)
The Poems of Jesus Christ

ANTHOLOGIES / EDITIONS

Modern European Poetry
Spanish Poetry from Its Beginnings through the Nineteenth
    Century
Eighteen Texts: Writings by Contemporary Greek Authors
Concrete Poetry: A World View (with Mary Ellen Solt)
A Book of Women Poets from Antiquity to Now
    (with Aliki Barnstone)
Borges at Eighty: Conversations
Literatures of Asia, Africa, and Latin America
    (with Tony Barnstone)
Literatures of the Middle East (with Tony Barnstone)

WILLIS BARNSTONE was born in Lewiston, Maine, and educated at Bowdoin, Columbia, and Yale. He taught in Greece at the end of the civil war (1949–51), in Buenos Aires during the Dirty War, and during the Cultural Revolution went to China, where he was later a Fulbright Professor of American Literature at Beijing Foreign Studies University (1984–1985). He has had more than seventy books published including, *Modern European Poetry* (Bantam, 1967), *The Other Bible* (Harper Collins, 1984), *The Secret Reader: 501 Sonnets* (New England, 1996), a memoir biography *With Borges on an Ordinary Evening in Buenos Aires* (Illinois, 1993), and *To Touch the Sky* (New Directions, 1999). His literary translation of the New Testament, *The New Covenant: The Four Gospels and Apocalypse* was published by Riverhead Books in 2002. His most recent publications include *Stickball on 88th Street, Café de l'Aube à Paris, Dawn Café in Paris: Poems Composed in French + Their Translation in English,* and *The Poems of Jesus Christ* (Norton, 2012).

A Guggenheim fellow, he has four times been nominated for the Pulitzer Prize in Poetry, and has had four Book of the Month Club selections. His poetry has appeared in *The Paris Review, The New Yorker, Poetry Magazine, The New York Review of Books,* and *The Times Literary Supplement.* His books have been translated into many languages including French, Italian, Romanian, Arabic, Korean, and Chinese. Barnstone lives in Oakland, California. A full-time writer he is also distinguished professor emeritus of comparative literature and biblical studies at Indiana University. He gives poetry readings, often with his daughter Aliki Barnstone and son Tony Barnstone.

TITLES FROM BLACK WIDOW PRESS

TRANSLATION SERIES

A Life of Poems, Poems of a Life
by Anna de Noailles. Translated by Norman R.
Shapiro. Introduction by Catherine Perry.

Approximate Man and Other Writings
by Tristan Tzara. Translated and edited by
Mary Ann Caws.

Art Poétique by Guillevic.
Translated by Maureen Smith.

The Big Game by Benjamin Péret.
Translated with an introduction by
Marilyn Kallet.

Capital of Pain by Paul Eluard.
Translated by Mary Ann Caws, Patricia Terry,
and Nancy Kline.

Chanson Dada: Selected Poems
by Tristan Tzara. Translated with an
introduction and essay by Lee Harwood.

*Essential Poems and Writings of
Joyce Mansour: A Bilingual Anthology*
Translated with an introduction by
Serge Gavronsky.

Essential Poems and Prose of Jules Laforgue
Translated and edited by Patricia Terry.

*Essential Poems and Writings of Robert Desnos:
A Bilingual Anthology*
Edited with an introduction and essay by
Mary Ann Caws.

EyeSeas (Les Ziaux) by Raymond Queneau.
Translated with an introduction by Daniela
Hurezanu and Stephen Kessler.

Furor and Mystery & Other Writings
by René Char. Edited and translated by
Mary Ann Caws and Nancy Kline.

The Inventor of Love & Other Writings
by Gherasim Luca. Translated by Julian and
Laura Semilian. Introduction by Andrei
Codrescu. Essay by Petre Răileanu.

La Fontaine's Bawdy by Jean de La Fontaine.
Translated with an introduction by Norman R.
Shapiro.

Last Love Poems of Paul Eluard
Translated with an introduction by
Marilyn Kallet.

Love, Poetry (L'amour la poésie) by Paul Eluard.
Translated with an essay by Stuart Kendall.

Poems of André Breton: A Bilingual Anthology
Translated with essays by Jean-Pierre Cauvin
and Mary Ann Caws.

Poems of A.O. Barnabooth by Valéry Larbaud.
Translated by Ron Padgett and Bill Zavatsky.

Poems of Consummation by Vicente Aleixandre.
Translated by Stephen Kessler.

Préversities: A Jacques Prévert Sampler
Translated and edited by Norman R. Shapiro.

The Sea and Other Poems by Guillevic.
Translated by Patricia Terry. Introduction by
Monique Chefdor.

To Speak, to Tell You? Poems by Sabine Sicaud.
Translated by Norman R. Shapiro. Introduction
and notes by Odile Ayral-Clause.

forthcoming translations

*Boris Vian Invents Boris Vian:
A Boris Vian Reader*
Edited and translated by Julia Older.

Pierre Reverdy: Poems Early to Late
Translated by Mary Ann Caws and
Patricia Terry.

Jules Supervielle: Selected Poems
Translated by Nancy Kline and Patricia Terry.

MODERN POETRY SERIES

WWW.BLACKWIDOWPRESS.COM